EPIDAUROS

AND MUSEUM

EDITION

THERA

G. VOUTSAS

ATHENS 1978

IMPRIME EN GRECE PAR VOUTSAS FRERES.
COPYRIGHT: C. VOUTSAS

ΑΝΑΠΑΡΑΣΤΑΣΙΣ ΤΟΥ ΙΕΡΟΥ ΤΟΥ ΑΣΚΛΗΠΙΟΥ

Wer zählt die Völker, nennt die Namen, Die gastlich hier zusammen - Kammen! (Schiller, Die Kraniche des Ibykus).

EPIDAUROS - ASKLEPIOS

ARCHAEOLOGICAL AND HISTORICAL PRESENTATION

The most famous theatre in antiquity was constructed on the slope of Mountain Kynortion, at a distance of 10 kms. from the coast of the Saronic Gulf. Just above the theatre, a narrow road leads to the architectural finds of earlier date, located and excavated by Greek archaeologists. They are the remains of a temenos which probably included the tomb of a hero worshipped in the tree - clad valley under the name of Maleas, or Apollo Maleatas, as he is often cited.

The surviving ancient ruins of the archaeological site of Epidauros belong principally to buildings of the 4th centyry B.C.

From that date and until the end of the Roman Imperial age, a cult was developed on the site. Traces of this cult are still encountered in our days in social life and in the therapeutic methods both scientific and practical.

Buildings of social utility and hotels, as well as countless votive monuments and exedrai were erected in the extended area of the sacred precinct. The temenos also included the Temple of Asklepios— with the chryselephantine (gold and ivory) statue of the god— the Temple of Artemis and the Temple of Isis.

The Tholos, a circular building of unusual architectural form and rich decoration, is particularly remarkable. The construction of the Tholos lasted 40 years (360 - 320 B. C.), and it is considered as one of the most elegant edifices of antiquity. (The Tholos of Delphi is an earlier construction, dating to the early 4th century B.C.).

The athletic and musical festivals celebrated every four years in honour of Asklepios, were performed in the Palaestra, the Gymnasium and the Stadium.

The temenos flourished principally during the 4th century B.C., not only because of the magnificent buildings which decorated the shrine at the time, but also because of the cult of Asklepios which was performed on the site.

Vast crowds of patients and pilgrims gathered in the sanctuary. The former slept in separate dwellings; during sleep, they were visited by the god, usually in the shape of a snake, who appeared to the ailing «in dream» and gave them instructions for their cure.

3

The numerous inscriptions, still preserved at present, provide examples of «prescriptions», «miracles» and cures of the god. Psychoneurotic disturbances were cured both by «shock» treatment and another psychiatric method, which was officially developed in Cos by Hippocrates and his disciples; the method was adopted later by the Christian religion and it has finally evolved into the so - called Psychotherapy of our times.

Asklepios became first known as a healing god in the ancient Greek world during the 5th century B.C., and was regarded since then as one of the most popular gods of the ancient Greeks. In 293 B.C., the cult of Asklepios spread to Rome, where the god appears with the same cult features and the same healing properties.

In Homer there is no special reference to the healing epiphany of the god Asklepios— as there is in Hesiod and Pindar— but the hero-sons of this infallible therapist are cited as physicians.

The cult of Asklepios seems to have originated at Trikke (the present-day Trikala in Thessaly), where he was in all probability worshipped as a hero - semigod for his healing powers.

A son of Coronis, daughter of Phlegyas, and Apollo, he is said to have been instructed by Cheiron, the wise Centaur of Pelion.

We learn about Asklepios' death from Hesiod and Pindar: he was struck by Zeus' thunderbolt, when Hades, the god of the nether world complained for the unequal number between the two worlds (the upper and the lower world) resulting from the miraculous intervention of the god, which diminished the number of the dead.

Asklepios was the husband of Epione and the father of Podaleirios and Machaon; he is usually represented accompanied by a snake or the well - known goddess Hygieia.

The Theatre: The Greek words «theatre», «chorus», «orchestra», «scene», are common among the theatrical circles of the whole world, meaning the same thing in different languages. The identification of the theatre with the ancient drama had already begun in Greece in the 6th century B.C.

The Theatre of Epidauros, visited and admired now as a work of art, is at the same time a complete and perfect architectural construction. Without losing the simplicity of the 6th century circular orchestra, in the middle of which stood the altar of Dionysos (Nietzsche, The Birth of Tragedy), it possesses a geometrical coherence that has been studied and recorded since the age of Augustus (Vitruvius, V, 7).

The employment of the area for the formation of a semicircular cavity, the «koilon» («cavea»), i.e. the place for the spectators, harmonizes well with the shape of the orchestra, which has a diameter of 9.77 m. The «kerkides», 55 in number, can accommodate approximately 14.000 spectators. The «koilon» («kerkides») is vertically and horizontally divided by stairs and «diazomata», in order to facilitate spectators in finding their seats. The honorary front row of seats was reserved for the officials («proedria») and lay just before the «euripos» which surrounded the orchestra. The «thymele» stood at the centre of the orchestra, at a distance of 22 m. from the highest tier and the retaining wall of the theatre. Before the orchestra and on either side of it, were the «parodoi» and «pylones, the «proskenion», the «logeion», the «paraskenia» and the «skene».

In recent years the construction of the theatre has been assigned to the early 3rd century B.C., and the addition of the epitheatre to the 2nd century B. C. This dating does not correspond with the information given by Pausanias, i.e. that Polykleitos erected the Theatre and the Tholos simultaneously, about the middle of the 4th century B. C. The theatre was lastly repaired in the 3rd century B. C., and later it was abandoned. Following the excavations by Greek archaeologists, the theatre has been partly restored. With its 55 tiers of seats, it offers the noble - minded spectators an opportunity to assist to a series of representations of ancient tragedies and comedies during the annual summer festival.

LIST OF ILLUSTRATIONS

6

Page 38
The Gymnasium

Page 38
The Katagogeion (hotel)

Page 39
A Corinthian capital from the Tholos, a work of the sculptor Polykleitos the Younger (370 B.C.); it had served as a model for the rest of the capitals of the peristyle. The "kalathos" is decorated with acanthus leaves arranged in two rows. The volutes seem to grow from the inner part of the leaves, and they support the abacus, thus giving the capital a quadrilateral form. Each of the four sides carries in the middle an anthemion ornament at the meeting point of the two smaller volutes.
This type of capital appears around the middle of the 5th century B.C., and its inspiration and execution are attributed to the sculptor Callimachos.

Page 40-41
Museum of Epidauros:
Members of the Tholos and sculptured decoration from other temples.

Page 42
A Corinthian capital from the Tholos, a work of the sculptor Polykleitos the Younger (370 B.C.); it had served as a model for the rest of the capitals of the peristyle. The «kalathos' is decorated with acanthus leaves arranged in two rows. The volutes seem to grow from the inner part of the leaves, and they support the abacus, thus giving the capital a quadrilateral form. Each of the four sides carries in the middle an anthemion ornament at the meeting point of the two smaller volutes.
This type of capital appears around the middle of the 5th century B.C., and its inspiration and execution are attributed to the sculptor Callimachos.

Page 43
Partial reconstruction of the Tholos, the most splendid edifice of the sacred shrine; its construction and decoration lasted 40 years (360-320 B.C.). A peristyle of 26 Doric columns (A) surrounded the circular sekos (B); in the sekos, another circular row of 14 exquisitely carved Corinthian colums (C) formed a small internal peribolos.

Page 44-45

Part of the lower section of the ceiling of the Tholos. The coffered ceiling presented a harmony of decorative ornaments having as central motif a rosette appearing amid acanthus leaves. In addition, the visitor must project with his imagination the phantasmagorically painted ceiling under the effect of light and shade, in order to form an image of the ancient Greek reality.

Page 46-47

The superb Tholos of Epidaurus is one of the most celebrated edifices of antiquity. The coffered ceiling was adorned with exquisitely carved rosettes and lilies, and the roof was supported by peristyles of Doric and Corinthian columns.

Page 47

Museum of Epidauros. On the right, copies of the statues of Asklepios and Hygieia. Museum of Epidauros: Partial reconstruction of the peristyle and ceiling of the Tholos.

Page 48-49

Part of the lower section of the ceiling of the Tholos. The coffered ceiling presented a harmony of decorative ornaments having as central motif a rosette appearing amidst acanthus leaves. In addition, the visitor must project with his imagination the phantasmagorically painted ceiling under the effect of light and shade, in order to form an image of the ancient Greek reality.

Page 50-51

Asklepios was most commonly represented standing and leaning on a staff with the sacred snake coiled around it. The god with thick hair and beard, wears only a himation which leaves most of his chest uncovered; he looks gentle and compassionate. The statue of Asklepios seen in this photograph, is exhibited in the National Archaeological Museum of Athens (Roman copy of the 2nd century A.D.); it is a representative specimen of the above type, the spreading and continuation of which reaches down to the 4th century A.D.

From the 5th century B.C., Asklepios was represented on votive reliefs, which were believed to possess the healing power of the god.

The chryselephantine cult statue of Asklepios, which represented the god seated on a throne, stood in the sanctuary of Epidauros; it was made by the sculptor Thracymedes in about 370 B.C.

Page 52

— Copy of a statue representing the goddess Hygieia (the original is in the National Archaeological Museum, Inv. No. 299). It comes from the Temple of Asklepios and it is partly damaged. The goddess bends to offer something to the sacred snake, part of which is visible at the lower section of the statue. From the movement of the legs and the bending of the body, the goddess seems to come out of an opening smaller than her height. This produces a masterly rendering in marble of the motion of the garment as related to that of the body. (Circa 380 B.C.).

Page 53

— Copy of a riding Amazon (the original is in the National Archaeological Museum, Inv. No. 136). It comes from the east pediment of the Temple of Asklepios, which was decorated with representations of fighting Amazons — a mythical warrior race of women dwelling N.E. of Asia Minor. (Circa 385 B.C.).

Page 54

A relief, votive (or architectural?). Upon a cushioned chair Asklepios is seated facing right, his feet crossed on a footstool. His bare chest is 3/4 facing; his face godlike. The palm of his left hand is open in benediction. A work in one of the leading sculptors of the pediment figures. About 380 B.C. (The head belongs to the relief, the opinion that it is alien is unsupported). Height of the old part 0.64 m., length without the restoration 0.47 m.

Page 54

From the same sculptor is the corresponding figure from the other corner of the pediment. The head is missing. Height 0.74 m., width 0.67 m.

Page 55

Acroterion of the temple of Asklepios. A beautiful woman, Nereid, Aura, of goddess, on a horse which emerges with its forefeet from the Ocean. The skillful pleating reveals the outline of her body. This, as well as her head, leans slightly toward the horse's neck. Hole for the application of the harness. Work of one of the principal sculptors of the temple. About 380 B.C. Height 0.78 m., width 0.66 m.

Page 56

Anthemion with astragal. The use of cymatia and anthemia expresses the artist's fine

talent and his intention for a careful execution and decorative enrichment of his work.
Detail of the interior peribolos of the Tholos.

Page 57
To the right and left of the visitor on entering the Museum, there are parts of the geison from the Propylaea and from the temple of Artemis.

Page 58
Museum of Epidauros. On the right, copies of the statues of Asklepios and Hygieia. Museum of Epidauros: Partial reconstruction of the peristyle and ceiling of the Tholos.

Page 59
The greatest number of votive offerings to Asklepios have been found in Corinth. Notable among the many ex-votos from Epidaurus are: the representation of a sick child; the theme of the child holding a little bird in the left hand is associated with the cult of Asklepios.

Page 60
The most remarkable of the statues representing a divine epiphany are:
a) the statue of the goddess Hygieia, the companion of the god Asklepios, with the sacred snake, sung in a hymn by Ariphron the Sikyonian in the 4th century B.C., and
b) the statue of the goddess Athena-Hygieia, whose cult was anterior to that of the companion of Asklepios. The Gorgon's head is visible on the aegis of Athena, while the sacred snake is coiled round the tree by her side. (Both statues are works of the Roman period.)

Page 61
The rich finds from the sanctuary of Epidaurus include many architectural components that had belonged to temples and other edifices. Among these are: part of the clay geison (awning) bearing a painted decoration of astragals, meanders and anthemia.

— Detail of an inscription citing the names of the craftsmen who had participated in the construction of the Temple of Asklepios and the Tholos and recording the labour and material expenses.

In about 300/280 B.C., the lyric poet Ioullos composed five poems, which have been identified in inscriptions found at Epidaurus. These include: the political beliefs of the poet (in trochaic tetrameter), thanksgiving to Apollo for having spared Sparta an invasion by Philip, father of Alexander the Great.

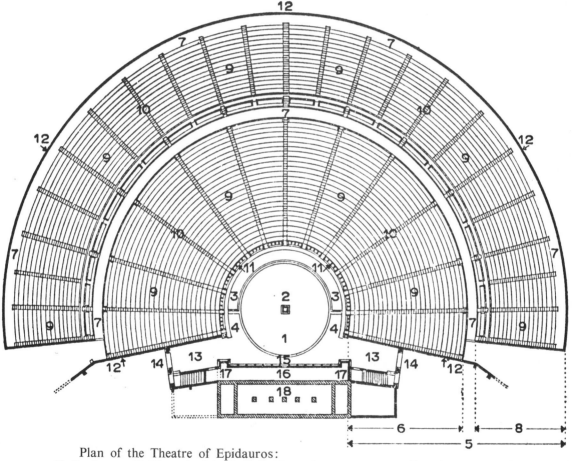

Plan of the Theatre of Epidauros:
1) Orchestra 2) Thymele (altar) 3) Euripos (passage surrounding the orchestra) 4) Descent 5) Koilon (auditorium) 6) Koilon 7) Diazomata (horizontal divisions of the koilon) 8) Koilon of the 2nd century B.C. 9) Kerkides (wedge - like sections) 10) Stairs 11) Proedria (seats of honour) 12) Retaining walls 13) Parodoi (side passages) 14) Pylones (gateways) 15) Proskenion (space in front of the skene) 16) Logeion (speaking-place) 17) Paraskenia spaces on either side of the skene) 18) Skene (stage).

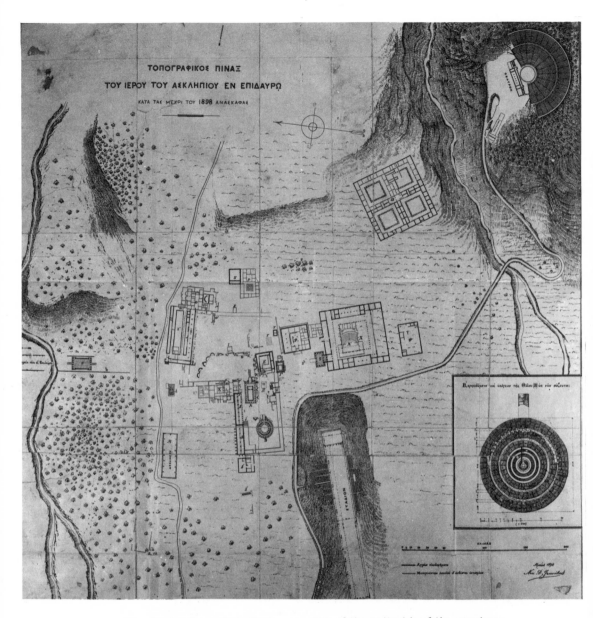

The Abaton (or enkoimeterion, i.e. stoa of the patients) of the sanctuary of Epidaurus belongs to the very ancient architectural type of stoas (arcades) 29 Ionic columns stood on the facade, while the stepsis rested on 13 columns on the interior. The stoa measured 9.50 m. in width and 70.00 m. in length, and served as sleeping quarters for the patients, awaiting the epiphany of the god Asklepios in their sleep.

L'«abaton» d'Epidaure (le portique des malades ou salle d'incubation) fait partie du très ancien type architectural des portiques. La facade avait 29 colonnes ioniques, tandis qu'á l'intérieur 13 colonnes supportaient le couronnement. Large de 9,50 m., long de 70,00 m. il abritait les malades qui attendaient l'apparition en songe du dieu Asclépios.

Der Abaton (oder Enkoimeterion, d.h. Krankenstoà) im Epidauros-Heiligtum ist eine Stoà (Säulenhalle), die eine der ältesten Architekturtypen ist. Die Fassade hatte 29 ionische Säulen. Im Innern standen 13 Säulen. Tiefe: 9.50 m, Länge: 70 m. Da hausten die Kranke, welche die Erscheinung des Gottes Asklepios im Traum erwarteten.

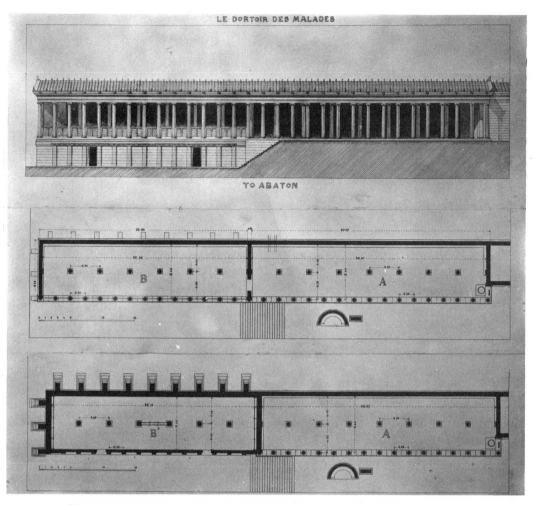

LE DORTOIR DES MALADES

TO ABATON

Topograpnical sketch Showing the site of anciet monuments in the Sanctuary of Asklepios:

Représentation topologique des monuments anciens du Sanctuaire d' Asslépios.

Topographische Darstellung alter Denkmäler des Asklepios-Heiligtums.

Bibliographie : U. V. Wilamovitz, Ysyllos von Epidaurus 1886. R.E. 2, 2 (1896), 1642 - 1697, F. Kutsch, Antiken Heilgötter und Heroen 1913. E. M. Edelstein, Asklepios, 1945. K. Kerenyi, der göttliche Arzt, 1948 und 1956. U. Hausmann, Kunst und Heiltum, 1948. W. Vollgraff, Le sanctuaire d'Apollon pythéen à Argos 1956, 55 ff. M. Bierer, Proc. of the American Phil. Society, 101, 1957, 70. EAA I 1958; 719 - 724 (Mansuelli). K. Shefold, Agorakritos in Festeschrift. R. Boehringen, 1957, 544 und Lexikon der Antiken (Religion-Mythologie), Band I, 125 ff. D. Herzog, Die Wunderheilungen von Epidaurus, 1931, F. Robert, Epidaure, 1935, J. Papadimitriou, Le Sanctuaire d'Apollon Maleatas à Epidaure, BCH. 73, 1949, 361 - 383.

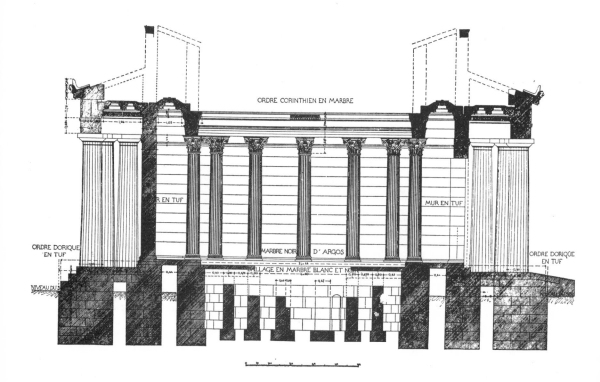

Epidauros, Tholos. – Nach A. Defrasse und H. Lechat, 1895.
Ausschnitt des Grundrisses mit spiegelbildlicher Untersicht der Kassettendecke.

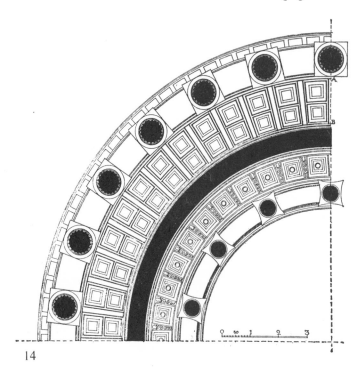

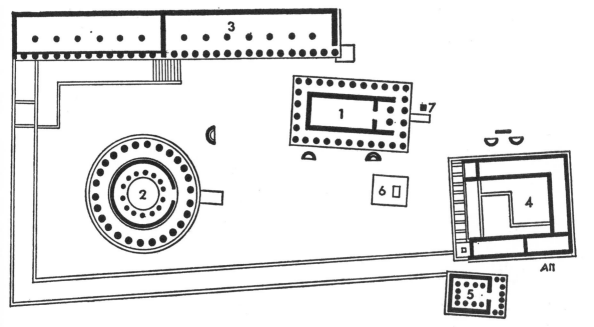

Sanctuary of Asclepios

The main buildings

1 Temple of Asclepios — 2 Tholos (Rotunda) — 3 Abaton or Enkoimeterion — 4 Ancient Abaton (?)
5 Temple of Artemis — 6 Great Altar of Asclepios — 7 Sacred Fountain

WAYS TO EPIDAUROS

1 : 1 800 000   1 cm = 18 km

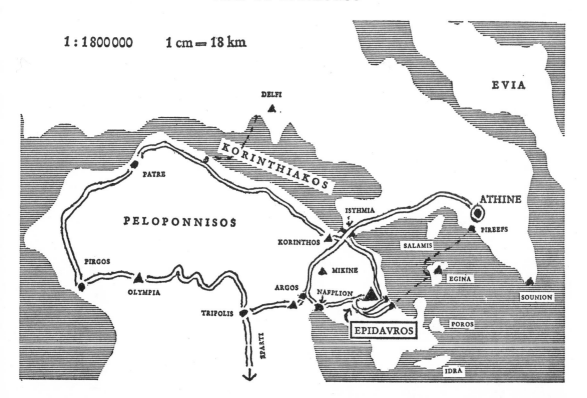

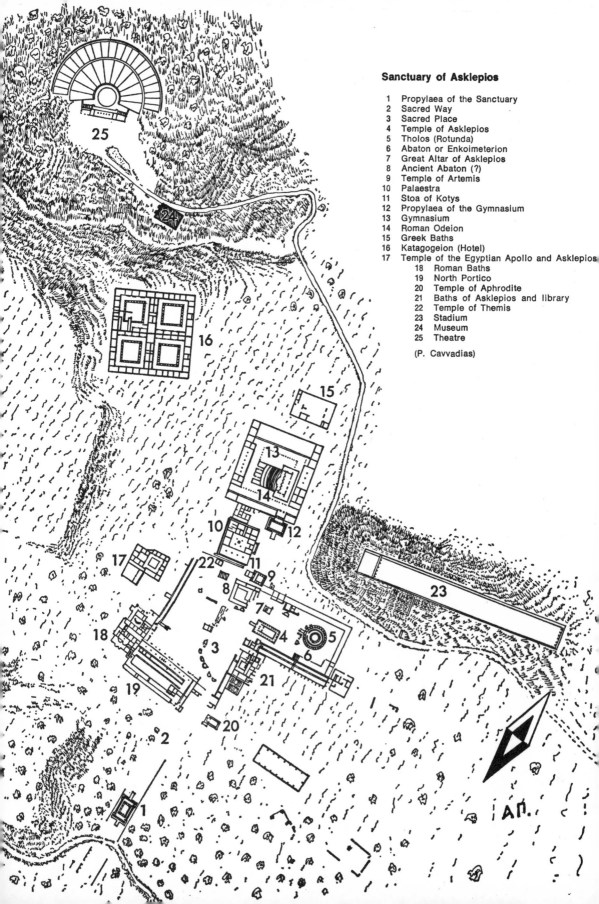

Sanctuary of Asklepios

1 Propylaea of the Sanctuary
2 Sacred Way
3 Sacred Place
4 Temple of Asklepios
5 Tholos (Rotunda)
6 Abaton or Enkoimeterion
7 Great Altar of Asklepios
8 Ancient Abaton (?)
9 Temple of Artemis
10 Palaestra
11 Stoa of Kotys
12 Propylaea of the Gymnasium
13 Gymnasium
14 Roman Odeion
15 Greek Baths
16 Katagogeion (Hotel)
17 Temple of the Egyptian Apollo and Asklepios
18 Roman Baths
19 North Portico
20 Temple of Aphrodite
21 Baths of Asklepios and library
22 Temple of Themis
23 Stadium
24 Museum
25 Theatre

(P. Cavvadias)

The Theatre   Le Théâtre   Das Theater

The theatre and the valley of Epidauros
Das Theater und das Tal von Epidauros
Le théâtre et la vallée d'Epidaure

The Theatre   *Le Théâtre*   *Das Theater*

20

The Orchestra of the Theatre
Die Orchestra des Theaters
L'orchestre du Théâtre

The Orchestra of the Theatre
Die Orchestra des Theaters
L'orchestre du Théâtre

Theatre of Epidauros: Air View.
Theatre d' Epidaure Vue aérienne.
Theater von Epidauros. Flugansicht.

22

The Sanctuary of Asklepios and the Theatre
Le Sanctuaire d'Asclépios et le Théâtre

Das Heiligtum des Asklepios und das Theater

General view of the Sanctuary from mount Titthion
Blick über den Heiligen Bezirk vom Berg Titthion aus
Vue générale du Sanctuaire, du haut du mont Titthion

25

The Theatre   *Le Théâtre*   *Das Theater*

The Propylaea of the San-
ctuary
Les Propylées du Sanctuaire
Die Propyläen des Heilig-
tums

The temple of Artemis
La temple d'Artémis

The Stadium   Das Stadion   Le Stade

The Tholos or Rotunda
Die Tholos oder Rotunde
La Tholos ou Rotonde

The Sanctuary of Asklepios
Le Sanctuaire d'Asclépios
Das Heiligtum des Asklepios

The Roman
Odeion

L'Odéon romain

Das römische
Odeon

The Gymna- Le Gymnase Das Gymnasium   sion

The Katagogeion (hotel)
Le Katagogeion (hôtel)
Das Katagogeion (Gasthof)

ΑΝΑΠΑΡΑΣΤΑΣΙΣ ΤΟΥ ΙΕΡΟΥ ΤΟΥ ΑΣΚΛΗΠΙΟΥ

Wer zählt die Völker, nennt die Namen, Die gastlich hier zusammen - Kammen! (Schiller, Die Kraniche des Ibykus).

EPIDAUROS
MUSEUM

Corinthian capital of the Tholos by Polykleitos the Younger
Korinthisches Kapitell der Tholos von Polyklet dem Jüngeren
Chapiteau corinthien de la Tholos par Polyclète le Jeune

The Museum's third room
Dritter Saal des Museums
La troisième salle du musée

Corinthian capital of the Tholos by Polykleitos the Younger
Korinthisches Kapitell der Tholos von Polyklet dem Jüngeren
Chapiteau corinthien de la Tholos par Polyclète le Jeune

Restored part of the Tholos (Rotunda)
Wiederherstellung eines Teils der Tholos (Rotunde)
Partie de la Tholos (Rotunde) restaurée

44 *Ceiling of the outer doric colonnade*
Kassettendecke des äuberen dorischen Säulengangs
Caissons du plafond de la colonnade dorique extérieure

Ceiling of the inner corinthian colonnade
Kassettendecke des inneren korinthischen Säulengangs
Caissons du plafond de la colonnade corinthienne intérieure

45

Ornaments of the ceiling of the inner colonnade (detail)
Verzierung der Kassettendecke des inneren Säulenganges (Detail)
Ornements des caissons du plafond de la colonnade intérieure (détail)

Ornaments of the ceiling of the outer colonnade
Verzierung der Kassettendecke des äuberen Säulenganges
Ornements des caissons du plafond de la colonnade extérieure ▶

The Museum's third room
Dritter Saal des Museums
La troisième salle du musée

Ornaments of the ceiling of the inner colonnade (detail)
Verzierung der Kassettendecke des inneren Säulenganges (Detail)
Ornements des caissons du plafond de la colonnade intérieure (détail)

Ceiling of the outer doric colonnade
Kassettendecke des äuberen dorischen Säulengangs
Caissons du plafond de la colonnade dorique extérieure

Ascklepios   *Asclépios*   *Asklepios*

Statue of the Goddess Hygieia
Statue der Göttin Hygieia
Statue de la déesse Hygie

Penthesile, central figure of the west perdiment of Asklepios' temple
Penthesilea, Zentralfigur des Westgiebels des Tempels des Asklepios
Penthésilée, figure centrale du fronton ouest du temple d'Asclépios

Ascklepios

Asclépios

Asklepios

Acroteria of the temple of Asklepios.
Nereids on horseback.

Acrotères du temple d'Asclépios.
Des Néréides à cheval.

Akroterien des Asklepiostempels.
Reitende Nereiden.

Acroteria of the temple of Asklepios. Nereids on horseback.
Acrotères du temple d'Asclépios. Des Néréides à che-
val.

Akroterien des Asklepiostempels. Reitende Nereiden.

55

Ornaments of the Tholos
Schmuckwerk der Tholos
Ornements de la Tholos

Entablature and corinthian column from the inner part of the Tholos
Gesims und korinthische Säule im inneren Teil der Tholos
Entablement et colonne corinthienne, partie intérieure de la Tholos

The temple of Artemis
La temple d'Artémis
Der Artemistempel.

The Museum's third room
Dritter Saal des Museums
La troisième salle du musée

*The representation of a sick child; the theme of the child holding a little bird
in the left hand is associated with the cult of Asklepios.
b) Une reproduction d'un enfant malade. Le thème de l'enfant tenant un petit
oiseau dans sa main gauche est relié au culte d'Asclépios.*

The statue of the goddess Athena - Hygieia.
La statue de la déesse Athéna - Hygie.
Statue der Göttin Athena-Hygieia.

The statue of the goddess Hygieia,
La statue de la déesse Hygie.
Statue der Göttin Hygieia.

Portrait heads of the Roman age, and male and female statues belong to Roman emperors, personifications of deities (e.g. Athena), or common mortals.

Bustes-portaits de l'époque romaine, statues d'hommes et de femmes, appartenant á des empereurs romains, á des représentations de divinités (p. ex. Athéna) et á de communs mortels.

Porträt-Büsten römischer Zeit, männliche und weibliche Statuen, römische Kaiserstatuen, Götterstatuen (u.a. Athena).

b) *Part of the clay geison (awning) bearing a painted decoration of astragals, meanders and anthemia.*

b) *le fragment d'une corniche en terre cuite á décoration peinte avec astragale, méandres et palmettes.*

b) *Gesimstragment aus Terracotta mit bemalten Astragalen, Meander und Palmetten.*

Inscription of expenses for the construction of Asklepios' Temple and the Tholos (detail)

Inschrift mit Baukostenaufzeichnung für den Tempel des Asklepios und die Tholos (Detail)

Inscription des dépenses pour la construction du temple d'Asclépios et de la Tholos (détail)

Paean to Asklepios and Apollo
Un paean á Asclépios et á Apollon
Paian zu Asklepios und Apollon.

ΕΠΙΠΕΩΣ ΓΙ ΔΙΑ ΑΝΤΙΟΧΟΥ

Μ ΙΟΥΛΙΟΣ ΑΠΕΛΛΑΣ ΙΔΡΙΕΥΣ ΜΥΛΑΣΕΥΣ ΜΕΤΕΠΕΜΦΘΗΝ
ΥΠΟ ΤΟΥ ΘΕΟΥ ΠΟΛΛΑΚΙΣ ΕΣ ΝΟΣΟΥΣ ΕΝΠΙΠΤΩΝ ΚΑΙ ΑΠΕΨΙ
ΑΙΣ ΧΡΩΜΕΝΟΣ ΚΑΤΑ ΔΗ ΤΟΝ ΠΛΟΥΝ ΕΝ ΑΙΓΕΙΝΗ ΕΚΕΛΕΥΣΕ Μ
ΜΕΜΠΙΠΟΛΛΑ ΟΡΓΙΖΕΣΘΑΙ ΕΠΕΙ ΑΓΕ ΤΕ ΝΟΜΗΝ ΕΝΙΟΙ ΣΕΡΟΣ
ΚΕΛΥΣΕΙΝ ΕΜΙ ΑΥΘΗΜΕΡΑΣ ΣΥΓΚΑΛΛΑΣ ΟΔΠΡΙΝ ΚΕΦΑΛΗΝ
ΠΝΑΙΣ ΟΜΒΡΟΙ ΓΕΝΟΝΤΟ ΕΥΡΩΝ ΚΑΙ ΑΠΙΟΝ ΙΡΟΛΑΚΕΝΕΣ Δ
ΝΑΜΕΤΑΦΡΙΔΑΣ ΑΥΤΟΝ ΔΙ ΑΥΤΟΥ ΛΟΥΣΘΑΙ ΔΜΟΥ ΓΥΜΝΑΣΙ
ΣΘΑΙ ΚΙΤΡΙΟΥ ΠΡΟΛΑΜΒΑΝΕΙΝ ΔΑΚΡΑΓΙΣ ΥΔΑΤΟ ΡΟΒΡΕΣ ΑΠΙΕΩ
ΠΑΙΣ ΑΚΟΑΙΣ ΕΝ ΑΝΘΙ ΟΤΙ ΓΡ ΥΠΡΕΣ ΟΛΛΙ ΟΙ ΤΟΙΧΟΙ ΠΕΡΙΠΑΤΩ ΧΩ
Ο ΘΑΛΥΠΕΡΟΥΩ ΣΠΑΙΣ ΑΦΗΜΙ ΙΑΛΟΣ ΔΣ ΟΛΙΑΝ ΥΠΟ ΛΗΤΟΝ ΤΕ ΡΙ
ΠΑΤΕΙΝ ΤΡΙΝΕΙ ΒΗΙΝΑΙ ΕΝΙ ΟΙΚΑΛΛΗ ΝΙ ΣΤΟ ΟΣ ΕΡΜΟΝ ΥΔΩΡ
ΟΙ ΝΟΝ ΠΡΙΧΕΑΣΘΑΙ ΜΟΝΟΝ ΔΝΟΥΣ ΔΣ ΘΑΙ ΚΑΤΑ ΔΙΚΗΝ ΔΥΝΑΙ
ΤΟΙ ΒΑΛΑΝΕΙ ΚΟΙΝΗ ΟΥΣ ΑΙΑΣ ΚΑΙ ΠΡΙΟΗ ΤΗ ΠΟΝ ΠΕΑΡΣ ΕΙΝΙΑΣ
ΓΑΛΑΜ Ε ΓΑΜ ΕΛΙΟΣ ΠΡΟΛΑΒΕΙΝ ΜΙΑΝ ΗΜΕΡΑ ΠΙΟΝΤΟΣ ΜΟΥ ΤΑ
ΛΑΜΒΟΝΟΝ ΕΠΙΕΝΜΕΑΙ ΕΜΒΑΛΛΕ ΙΣ ΤΟΓΑΛΛΙΝΑ ΛΥΝΗ ΠΑΙΑ ΝΑ
ΠΤΕΙΝΕ ΠΕΙΛΕΕΓΑ ΠΘΟΗ ΝΤΟΥ ΘΕΟΥ ΘΑΤΟΝ ΜΕΛΠΟΑΣ ΑΙΟΜΕΝΑ
ΠΥΚΝΑΔΣ ΙΝ ΚΣ ΧΡΕΙΜΕΝΟΣ ΟΛΟΣ ΕΠΕΙΝΑΙ ΚΑΙ ΑΓΑΚΟΑΣ ΕΚΣ Υ
ΑΒΑΤΟΥ ΠΑΙΑΛΛΟΝ ΑΓΗΙ ΣΙΣ ΟΛΙΘ ΥΜΙ ΑΤΗ ΡΙΟΝ Ε ΧΟΝΑΙ ΜΕΓΟ
ΡΑΠΙΟΝΙ ΕΓΡΑΛΕΠΕ ΠΝΙ ΘΕΡΑΠΕΥΣΑΙ ΧΡΗ ΔΕ ΑΠΟΜΙΔΟΝΑ ΠΑΡΑΓΡΑ
ΚΑΙ ΠΟΙΗΣΑΣ ΙΑΛΟΝ ΚΑΙ ΧΡΕΙΜΕΝΟΣ ΜΕΝΤΟΙ ΑΛΛΑ ΙΚΑΙ ΤΟΙΝ ΑΥ
ΧΙΕΒΟΙ ΗΛΑΙΣ ΑΛΛΟΥ ΜΕΝΟΣ ΔΕ ΟΥΚ ΗΛΤΗΣ ΑΤΑΥΤΑΙ ΕΝΤΝΝΙ ΑΠΕΙ
ΑΙΣ ΑΦΟΥ ΗΑ ΟΝ ΗΣΑ ΤΟΛΕΜΟΥ ΚΑΤΗΣ ΔΕΞΙ ΑΣ ΧΙΡΟΣ ΚΑΙ ΘΥ
ΣΙΑΣ ΤΟ ΣΠΑΣ ΕΝΙ ΣΗ ΜΕΡΑ ΠΕΙΟΥ ΝΤΟΣ ΜΟΥ ΦΑΣ ΑΝΑΛΑΡΟ Ν
ΣΑ ΕΠΙ ΤΟ ΛΕΥΣ ΕΠΙ ΝΧΕΙΡΑΟΣ ΚΑΙ ΦΛΥΚΤΑΙΝΑ ΣΤΕ ΑΝ ΟΙΣΛΑΙ ΤΟ
ΛΙΤΟΝΔΕ ΥΠΕΙΣΙ ΧΕΙΡΕ ΤΕ ΝΕ ΟΕΤΙ ΜΕ ΙΝΑΝ ΤΙ ΜΟΙ ΑΝ ΕΘΟΝΕ
ΓΕΛΛΙΟΥ ΧΡΗΣΑΣΘΑΙ ΤΟΣ ΤΗ ΝΚ ΕΦΑΛΑ ΤΙ ΑΝ ΕΠΙ ΓΕΝΟΜΙ ΡΙΝ ΑΙ
ΙΟΥΝ ΤΗΝ ΚΕΦΑΛΗΝ ΣΥΝΕΒΗ ΟΥΝ ΦΙΛΑΛΟΦΗΣ ΑΝΤΙ ΠΟΙΣ ΟΠΙ ΤΑ
ΙΩΘΗ ΝΑ ΤΧΡΗΣΑΜΕΝΟΣ ΤΩ ΕΛΛΑ ΙΩΑ ΤΗΑΛΔΙΝΤΕΣ ΧΕ ΦΑΛΛΑ ΝΙ
ΑΣ ΑΝ ΑΓΑ ΤΑΡΙΣΙΣ ΟΛΝ ΥΧΕΟΤΙ ΠΡΟΣ ΤΙΝΕ ΤΑΦΥΛΠΙ ΚΑΙ ΓΑΡ ΠΕ ΤΙ
ΤΟΥ ΤΟΥ ΠΑΕΓΚΑ ΛΕΣ Α ΤΟΝ ΘΕΟΝ ΤΟ ΛΥΣ ΟΚΑΠ ΠΟΣ ΤΑΡΙΣΘΗΙ ΑΕΚΙ
ΛΕΥΣΕ ΠΙ ΔΕ ΚΑΙ ΑΝΑΤΡΑ ΨΑΠ ΤΑΥΤΑΧΑΡΙΝ ΕΙΛΟΣ ΚΑΙ ΥΓΠΣΕ ΣΕ
      ΝΟΜΕΝΟΣ ΑΠΠΗΛΛΑ ΓΗΝ

Apellas' inscription on his cure
Inschrift mit Bericht über die Heilung des Apellas
Inscription d'Apellas concernant sa guérison